# Caregiver Devotions

30 quick devotions for caregivers
to strengthen & explore their
personal relationship with God
between doctor appointments &
trying to catch their breath

I0558700

**Lisa Marie Heath**

Author of *Life of Lisa: Overcoming Adversity
With Love and Laughter*

# Caregiver Devotions

is a work of my own creation.

The information in this book was correct at the time of publication, and the Author does not assume any liability for loss or damage caused by errors or omissions, again, this is my perspective, opinion, and experience, so it has been written as such.

ISBN - 9781961185876

Cover, Book Design, and Layout by megs thompson
megswrites llc - *www.megswrites.com*

*www.inomniaparatuspublishing.com*

# Hello Caregivers!

**One of the hardest jobs on earth, in my opinion, is being a caregiver in any way. I see you. I recognize your struggles. Why? Because I'm a caregiver too.**

As caregivers, we're constantly focused on being everything to everyone else. When it comes to finding balance between caring for others & caring for ourselves, it can feel nearly impossible. And good luck trying to find the time to strengthen & explore your relationship with the man upstairs.

When we do find that time, it can be difficult or frustrating. Trying to make sense of what the Good Book & God are trying to tell us can be seriously overwhelming.

Which is why I've created **Caregiver Devotions**. 30 quick **daily devotions with verses** restyled in a way that makes sense to the modern caregiver, along with a **prayer** written especially for us to restart a conversation with God.

Do yourself a favor, please. After reading each devotion, promise me that you'll take three deep breaths & try to reflect on what you've read before diving back into your day.

**Your life, is no accident. No matter how messy it may seem. God, the Father, the ultimate caregiver has a plan for you, for each of us. *Trust me on this!***

XOXO

Lisa

# Sacred

Show up with love for the ones who raised you, whether it's hugs, home-cooked meals, or helping set up their Wi-Fi. Caring for your parents isn't just a nice thing; you're continuing the circle of care, and that's sacred work.

Exodus 20:12  LOLV

**Prayer:**

God, It can be hard at times. Please allow my actions to provide assistance to my loved ones & anyone in my care. Thank you for allowing me to be a part of the sacred circle of life. In your name. Amen.

# Load

When you take the time to help someone carry their load, you do God's work. Caregiving is the epitome of Christ-like living.

**Galatians 6:2 LOLV**

**Prayer:**

Dear God, Thank you for showing up in me & my life. After I have given my all & the loads I carry feel heavier than ever, that is when I'm reminded that you are always with me & that I'm never carrying any of this alone. I'm blessed to have you beside me, every step of the way. In your name. Amen.

# Love

Love isn't just saying 'I care.' It's midnight medicine runs, warm meals & showing up when it's inconvenient. And that? That's the real kind of love.

1 John 3:18 LOLV

**Prayer:**

Lord, Showing up when I don't want to is hard. Sometimes it feels like I'm the only one here to help, run errands & deal with the messy stuff. But I know that these are all opportunities for me to show your love, real love, for those around me. Thank you for always loving me, *really* loving me & allowing me to share that love with others. Amen.

# Forgive

Being kind, soft-hearted & able to forgive quickly is basically the caregiver starter pack.

**Ephesians 4:32 LOLV**

**Prayer:**

Lord, Please help to calm my voice & allow me to remember that those I care for are not seeking to anger & frustrate me. They're struggling with their own circumstances & my role is to share your unwavering love with them, even when things are rough. With your help, I strive to have a soft heart, a kind laugh & to forgive often. In your name. Amen.

# Advocate

Speak up for those without a voice. Advocacy is caregiving with a megaphone.

Proverbs 31:8-9 LOLV

**Prayer:**

Dear Heavenly Father, It's not always easy to know what to say, when to say it, or how. Please help me to use my words in ways that communicate your voice, message, and love with those who need to hear it most. In your name. Amen.

 # Friend

A true friend sticks around in the mess. A real one shows up when things get really tough.

**Proverbs 17:17 LOLV**

**Prayer:**

Dear God, Thank you for always being a true friend. Not just to me, but to those in my care. I do my best to follow your lead & stick around through the hard times as well as show up when things are tough. But it can be a struggle. There are times when all I want to do is hide under the covers in the quiet of my own room. Please help give me the strength to be a real friend to those in need. Amen.

# Care

Love big, love deep & love like Jesus, without holding back. When you care for someone, you show them a love that helps soothe the craziness of the world.

John 13:34 LOLV

**Prayer:**

Dear Heavenly Father, Your love has been a guiding light in my life for as long as I can remember. I try my best to love like you do, not just my family & friends, but those who are in my care & strangers I meet throughout the day. It can be difficult though. When I'm exhausted, stressed & completely out of compassion. Please fill me up with your love so that I can share it with others. Amen.

# Mercy

When you lead with compassion, even when you're running on fumes, you're not just being kind. You're inviting kindness back to you. Mercy is a Godly boomerang.

**Matthew 5:7 LOLV**

**Prayer:**

Lord, thank you for always reminding me that compassion matters, even when I feel like I've got nothing left to give. Some days I'm running on nothing, but I still want to lead with love. Please refill my tank with mercy & kindness. Help me trust that what I pour out will come back to me in Your perfect way. Amen.

# Strength

Sometimes caregiving means biting your tongue, taking a breath & forgiving...*again*. It's not a weakness, though, it's strength wrapped in grace.

Colossians 3:13 LOLV

**Prayer:**

God, you know how hard it is to keep forgiving when the same buttons are being pushed again & again. Please help me to pause, breathe & choose grace instead of resentment. Strengthen my spirit so that my forgiveness reflects Your love. Not my weakness, but quiet, steady strength wrapped in grace. Amen.

 # Selfless

When you put someone else's needs ahead of your own, especially on the really hard days, that's real love. The kind that changes lives *(including yours)* & the entire world.

John 15:13 LOLV

**Prayer:**

Dear Heavenly Father, as I take care of others, please take care of me. It's a struggle sometimes to face the unknown. God, my life is different but unique, just as you made me & I love that. There are times, like today, when I'm tired, stressed & pushed past my limits. I still know in my heart that I'm the best person for this job. Amen.

# Emotions

Hey, caregiver, you don't have to carry it all alone. Drop that emotional load at God's feet. He's built to carry the really heavy stuff.

Psalm 55:22 LOLV

**Prayer:**

Heavenly Father, Sometimes the weight of my emotions, worry & exhaustion feels like it's too heavy for me to hold. Help me remember to lay it all at Your feet & trust You to handle the heavy stuff. I know You've got me, always. In your name, Amen.

# Comfort

God fills you with comfort so you'll always have something to pour into others. When it feels like you're running on empty, you're actually running on divine-grade fuel.

2 Corinthians 1:4 LOLV

**Prayer:**

Lord, thank You for filling me up with comfort, even when I don't know I'm being refueled. When I feel like I'm running on empty, remind me that You're my source of divine-grade energy. Let Your peace & love flow through me so I can pour it into others. In your name, Amen.

# Gifts

Your gift, whether that's patience, humor, or ninja-level caregiving, isn't random. You were hand-picked by God to receive it & believe it or not, you're using those skills like a pro.

1 Peter 4:10 LOLV

**Prayer:**

Dear God, thank You for the gifts You've placed in me. Patience, humor, compassion & all the rest. Some days I doubt myself, but You remind me that I was chosen on purpose for this work. Help me to keep using these gifts you've given me with confidence & joy, knowing that I'm doing Your work with my hands & heart. Amen.

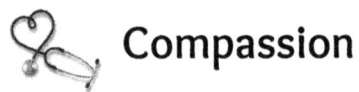

# Compassion

Whether you're wiping tears, changing bedding, or brewing a pot of tea, let love & compassion be the motivation for why you do what you do. *FYI, it's your secret superpower.*

### 1 Corinthians 16:14 LOLV

**Prayer:**

Lord, may everything I do today, big or small, be done with compassion. Whether I'm comforting, cleaning, cooking, or simply showing up, let compassion be my why. Fill my actions with warmth & grace so that others can feel Your presence through my care. In your name. Amen.

# Grace

Treat others how you'd want to be treated on the worst day ever. That means patience, grace & zero judgment. That's the good stuff.

**Leviticus 19:18 LOLV**

**Prayer:**

Dear Heavenly Father, please help me treat others with the same care & kindness I'd want to receive on my hardest day. Give me patience, gentleness & maybe a reminder or two to offer others snacks, and grace in equal measure. Let my love be practical, pure & pleasing to You. Amen.

# Energy

Feel like you're running on empty? Good news! God's in the energy business. He'll never let you run out. *In my opinion, power naps are definitely still an option.*

Isaiah 40:29 LOLV

**Prayer:**

Dear Heavenly Father, thank You for being my constant source of strength & energy. When my tank is low, I trust that you will continue to refill me, even if I don't recognize it. When I do rest, help me to not feel guilty, allow me to recharge in your presence & rise again ready to serve with energized love. In your name. Amen.

# Support

God is always your built-in backup support system. When life feels like it's in chaos, *I'm sure it is,* but He's your calm in the storm. All you have to do is give him a call.

Psalm 46:1 LOLV

**Prayer:**

Lord, when life feels chaotic & loud, thank You for being my safe harbor. My personal security guard & my steady place when everything else is shaking. Help me to pause, breathe & remember that You are always just a prayer away—ready to help, steady & strong. In your name. Amen.

 # Hard

You can do hard things. You already are & you're not doing it alone.

**Philippians 4:13 LOLV**

**Prayer:**

Dear God, I have a confession. Sometimes I don't want to do hard things. I just want to hide from the world & not deal with anything or anyone. Please strengthen my will so I can do the things that have to be done. Thank you for never leaving me alone. In your name, Amen.

# Cheer

You're never flying solo in life. God's right beside you, always cheering you on & holding you up, like a good squad.

Isaiah 41:10 LOLV

**Prayer:**

Dear God, thank You for walking right beside me & cheering me on, even when I can't feel You there. Some days I stumble & fall flat on my face, but You're always there, pulling me back up with cheer & grace. Please help me to feel Your presence & draw courage from Your steady love. In your name, Amen.

# Break

Psst. You're allowed to take breaks. Jesus said so. Let Him carry the stress for a moment or two. He's got the stronger shoulders.

**Matthew 11:28–30 LOLV**

**Prayer:**

Dear Heavenly Father, thank You for reminding me to rest. Sometimes I forget that I'm allowed to stop, to breathe & to let You carry the heavy load for a while. Please help me to hand over my stress & weariness, trusting whole-heartedly that Your shoulders & Your heart, can handle it all. Amen.

# Heartache

On days when your heart aches &
your soul feels squashed, God is
closer than close. Right there in the
middle of the mess beside you,
holding your hand & helping you
catch your breath.

**Psalm 34:18 LOLV**

**Prayer:**

Dear God, on the days when my heart
feels broken & my soul aches, thank
You for being close. Please help me
to feel Your nearness in the middle of
the mess. Hold my hand, steady my
breath & remind me I'm never alone
in my pain or heartache. In Your
Name. Amen.

 **Divine Love**

You're loving & caregiving like you are because God loved you first. You are passing along divine love to all of those you meet, like a divinely inspired relay race.

1 John 4:19 LOLV

**Prayer:**

Dear Heavenly Father, thank You for loving me and filling my cup when I need it the most. The love in my heart flows directly from you into me, and then others. Help me to keep passing your divine love forward with grace, compassion & joy, one person at a time. Amen.

# Serve

Every bath drawn, every lunch made, every load of laundry folded; you are never serving *just* one person. You're loving on Jesus Himself & he appreciates every moment of your care.

Matthew 25:40 LOLV

**Prayer:**

Dear Lord, thanks for the reminder that every small act of care matters. When I serve others, I'm serving You. Help me to approach *even* the simplest tasks, like the verse says, with love and gratitude, knowing that You see & cherish it all. Amen.

 # Time

Keep your love on the front burner. When you provide care for someone else with your time that's God-level love. The really good stuff.

**Romans 12:10 LOLV**

**Prayer:**

Dear God, help me keep love at the center of everything I do at all times. Let my care be patient, my words gentle & my heart open. May every act of service reflect Your deep & holy love, the kind that changes everything. Amen.

# Seeds

Hey Caregiver, you're tired, I get it, but don't give up. The seeds you sow in love will always blossom. Just keep watering.

**Galatians 6:9 LOLV**

**Prayer:**

Lord, sometimes I feel bone-tired & wonder if what I'm doing even matters. Please remind me that every act of love plants a seed & those seeds will bloom in Your time. Give me the strength to keep showing up, to keep watering & to trust Your beautiful harvest. Amen.

# Passion

Even the not-so-glamorous tasks, like sorting meds & cleaning up the gross stuff? It's still heavenly work. Do it with passion, like it's for God, because (*spoiler alert*) it is.

**Colossians 3:23–24 LOLV**

**Prayer:**

Dear God, Please help me to stay passionate about serving others, even when it means taking care of the disgusting & monotonous tasks that I despise. Help me to remember that everything I do, I'm doing in your name. I know that by sharing my love with others, I am sharing your love with those who need it most, often when they need it. most. Please continue to give me the strength I need. In your name. Amen.

# Heal

You're never alone in tending wounds. God's the original Healer. He's beside you every step of the way, hand in hand, heart to heart.

Psalm 147:3 LOLV

**Prayer:**

Dear Heavenly Father, Sometimes it can feel like I'm fighting a losing battle against the devil. Trying my best to help and soothe those in my care. Please help me to remember that I am never alone. You are always with me, beside me, using my hands and heart to care for your children. In your name. Amen.

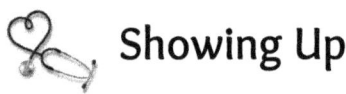

# Showing Up

When you show up for someone sick or struggling, God shows up for you. Just as you care for them, He cares for you. No ifs, ands, or buts.

**Psalm 41:1–3 LOLV**

**Prayer:**

Hey God, thank You for showing up for me the way I *really* try to show up for others. When I'm worn out & discouraged, help me remember that You see all of my effort & care for me in return. Your love restores me so that I can keep loving others too. Amen.

# Trust

Every act of caregiving is a love note to God. He sees & trust me, He does love you too.

**Hebrews 13:16 LOLV**

**Prayer:**

Dear Lord, the unseen acts of care, quiet gestures of patience & every bit of love that I pour out are my offerings to You. I trust that You see it all. Amen.

 # Identity

As a caregiver, you might sometimes feel invisible, but God sees your every single move. Nothing is ever wasted or forgotten.

1 Corinthians 15:58 LOLV

**Prayer:**

Lord, there are days when I wake up feeling like I've lost myself. I'm shrinking away, becoming invisible & completely losing all sense of my identity. It feels like my body & heart are being weighed down by the world, filled to the limit with worry for my loved ones. Please continue to wrap your arms around us all & fill me with your peace, reminding me that nothing is ever forgotten. In your name. Amen.

# About the Author

Lisa Marie Heath is the inspiring & lighthearted woman behind multiple inspiring books, a public speaker & an advocate for individuals living with TBIs as well as their caregivers.

Through her warm, conversational style, Lisa connects with audiences & readers by blending humor, vulnerability & thought-provoking reflections. Her work explores themes of self-discovery, drawing readers into an intimate journey of authenticity & hope.

When Lisa isn't writing, she enjoys connecting with her community, giving back & soaking up the beauty of life's small moments—whether that's relaxing poolside, gardening with her dad, or enjoying a few well-earned quiet sunny days at the beach.

For more information about Lisa's story, additional titles & how you can book Lisa to speak on your podcast or at your next event, visit her website at
*www.lifeoflisaheath.com.*

'